Ignite Your Generosity

A 21-Day Experience in Stewardship

NOW WITH SMALL GROUP GUIDE

Chris McDaniel
Foreword by **Dan Busby**

IVP Books

An imprint of InterVarsity Press
Downers Grove, Illinois

InterVarsity Press
P.O. Box 1400, Downers Grove, IL 60515-1426
ivpress.com
email@ivpress.com

InterVarsity Press® is the book-publishing division of InterVarsity Christian Fellowship/USA®, a movement of students and faculty active on campus at hundreds of universities, colleges and schools of nursing in the United States of America, and a member movement of the International Fellowship of Evangelical Students. For information about local and regional activities, visit intervarsity.org.

Cover design: Cindy Kiple
Images: ©pay404/iStockphoto

ISBN 978-0-8308-4431-9 (print)
ISBN 978-0-8308-9877-0 (digital)

Printed in the United States of America ∞

 As a member of the Green Press Initiative, InterVarsity Press is committed to protecting the environment and to the responsible use of natural resources. To learn more, visit greenpressinitiative.org.

Library of Congress Cataloging-in-Publication Data
Library of Congress Control Number: 2015930922

P 22 21 20 19 18 17 16 15 14 13 12 11 10 9 8 7 6 5 4 3 2

Y 34 33 32 31 30 29 28 27 26 25 24 23 22 21 20 19 18 17 16 15

CONTENTS

FOREWORD

This book is for those who desire to better understand the wonderful experiences the Bible offers when we grow in the grace of giving.

Ignite Your Generosity is easy to read and you'll find simple ways to apply your new learning. The book is divided into three sections:

1. What Does God Want You to Know? (Days 2–6)

2. What Does He Want You to Do? (Days 7–17)

3. Ignite the Fire! (Days 18–21)

Each section has short readings so that, in only a few minutes a day, you can digest this book over a three-week period. You could read it in a couple of hours rather than three weeks, but I highly encourage you to take the time. Answer the questions that are placed throughout. It will help you process what you are reading—by moving it from your mind to your heart and your hands. By interacting with the reading, you'll begin to experience the transforming power of God's Word made real in your own life.

Ignite Your Generosity is not merely another devotional. It will help you to develop your practical and personal theology for generous giving. At the same time, you are being transformed on your own journey, both through the formational exercises and your own experience. It provides a clear road map for the Christian's generosity journey. I most highly recommend it to you. May God continue to develop your heart as a cheerful giver! (2 Corinthians 9:7)

Dan Busby, president, ECFA

INTRODUCTION

The God of the Bible is radically generous. As followers of Christ we resemble him most when we are living generously. Many give out of obligation or guilt, yet biblical generosity is a generosity that flows from our love of God and our desire to be generous as Christ is generous. My prayer is that you will find the time to get away and connect with God on this very important topic and allow the Holy Spirit to be your guide. I also pray that these tools open the door of discussion about a topic that is not often addressed.

Ignite Your Generosity has been updated and expanded and now offers four resources to help you grow:

1. ***Ignite Your Generosity.*** Twenty-one daily devotionals with reflection questions and space for journaling. The devotional is designed for an individual to go deep with God on the topic of stewardship and generosity.

2. **Small Group Guide.** Included as an the appendix to *Ignite Your Generosity*, this resource offers four weekly readings with questions and activities designed for small groups on the following topics: Living as Exiles, Giving Cheerfully, Giving Sacrificially and Giving Regularly.

3. **Generosity Challenge.** An exciting, free resource, with twenty-seven daily challenges to complete after using the *Ignite Your Generosity* resource and the *Small Group Guide*, available at ivpress.com/ignite. Each challenge provides Scripture passages to consider and space for reflection and prayer requests.

4. **The Stewardship Bookmark** (sold separately). A quick reference tool that churches and ministries can purchase in bulk and give away to help readers remember the key concepts and Scriptural principles from the *Ignite Your Generosity* journey. This tool can be carried and stored in a Bible or notebook to serve as an ongoing reminder of the journey of stewardship that never ends, while also debunking some of the most prevalent lies about stewardship. Learn more at stewardship bookmark.org.

How to use

A journey through *Ignite Your Generosity* is most effective within the context of community.

While this journey can take many shapes, one idea is for each member of a local church to read and work through the *Ignite Your Generosity* devotional while simultaneously meeting weekly in small groups to discuss the four important topics covered in the *Small Group Study Guide*. Each topic is designed to be read aloud or privately during group time with a facilitator taking the group through the questions and next steps.

After participants complete the *Ignite Your Generosity* guide, they can visit ivpress.com/ignite and download the free *Generosity Challenge*. I recommend that participants work through the challenges individually then share the struggles, successes and "God-stories" that take place along the way with their small groups. Participants can pray for each other through the struggles and praise God for what he is doing in and through each person as they respond in obedience to him.

May God be with you as you ignite your generosity in response to his faithfulness, mercy and love.

> *Then the way you live will always honor and please the Lord, and your lives will produce every kind of good fruit. All the while, you will grow as you learn to know God better and better.*
>
> *Colossians 1:10 (New Living Translation)*

DAY 1

BEING A MIRACLE

When I was in my early 20s, I started working for a little Christian radio station where they couldn't pay me much. I got a very modest salary with one little benefit—a company vehicle.

So I thought I could get a little more cash by selling my own car. I put it in the paper and week after week after week went by. Nobody was interested.

So I started to pray that God would sell my car, and one day as I was praying about this, I heard this whisper, "So what are you going to do with the money if I sell your car?"

"Spend it!" was my first thought, but then all of a sudden I saw a vivid image of a coworker's family. I worked with the guy. They were a couple my parents' age with two kids close to my own age. And I knew that they were having an excruciating time financially.

They had one income and it wasn't very big. They were living in this little rented house and they had some health issues. These people were just getting bowled over by circumstances in their lives. So I said, "OK, God, if you sell my car, I'll give a sizeable portion to this family." The number that popped into my head was at least double, maybe triple, anything that I'd ever given away before. It was a lot of money for me.

So this is not going to surprise you, but right afterwards, my car sells. So, I say, "So, God, you know when we were talking about that whole agreement thing? Well . . . OK, OK, I'm good for it!"

I went to the bank, cashed the check and put the wad of money in an envelope and waited till it got dark. I drove over to the street where their house was, and it's funny, this happened fifteen years ago and I still remember it so clearly. I parked several houses away, sneaked out to this mailbox, opened it, stuffed the envelope in, closed it and dashed to my car.

The next day at work this man had a bunch of people gathered around him and he was sobbing, just sobbing. He held up the envelope, and said, "Darren, look at this, look what God gave me."

Funny—he was calling it a miracle. That God gave him this money. I remember the look on his face, I remember thinking so clearly, "Yes . . . God did give you that money. Wow, I got to be a part of a miracle!"

(Darren Whitehead, Church of the City, Nashville)

Have you ever been used by the God of the Universe? If so, you know that there's nothing like it. The adrenaline kicks in. Every fiber, every nerve is alive, on fire. Think of the most exciting thing that you've ever done—and it pales in comparison.

A deep sense of awe came over them all, and the apostles performed many miraculous signs and wonders. . . . They sold their property and possessions and shared the money with those in need . . . all the while praising God and enjoying the goodwill of all the people. And each day the Lord added to their fellowship those who were being saved.

Acts 2:43, 45, 47 (New Living Translation)

That's what He's calling you to do. He's inviting you to climb out of the stands—to quit watching—to suit up and get in the game. He has a jersey with your name on it, ready to give to you. He has hand-selected you—do you think that you're reading this book by accident?

Henry Blackaby says in *Experiencing God* that when you see Him working—when you sense Him drawing you toward something—*that is your invitation to join Him.*[1]

So . . .

this is it.

This is your invitation.

Are you ready?

It will be the ride of your life. It will ignite something in you that you didn't know existed.

You will do things you never dreamed of.

You will see the impossible.

---

[1] Henry Blackaby and Claude V. King, *Experiencing God*, (Nashville: Broadman & Holman, 1998), p. 35.

Stop.
Just sit there.
Drink this in.

And then, when you're ready . . .
What's going on in your heart?
In your mind?

What's God saying to you?
How do you want to respond?

Part One

What Does God Want You To Know?

DAY 2

WHOSE MONEY IS IT ANYWAY?

Today I was looking at a map-of-the-world placemat I got for my kids. There are some interesting observations one can make beneath the dried, spattered spaghetti sauce . . .

Everybody wants to own something.

There's an island west of Mexico that France owns.

The Caribbean islands are owned by the U.S., U.K., France and the Netherlands.

The U.K. owns lots of islands just north of Antarctica, and Norway owns one there as well.

Other islands scattered about the planet are owned by India, New Zealand, Australia, Spain, Portugal, Japan and more. There are even rumors that some islands belong to people who were living there in the first place.

There is also an international best-selling author who buys islands. He has acquired four of them, ranging from the coast of Ireland to the coast of Australia.

So who really owns it all?

The One who created it all.

> *. . . for every animal of the forest is mine, and the cattle on a thousand hills. I know every bird in the mountains, and the creatures of the field are mine . . . for the world is mine, and all that is in it.*
>
> Psalm 50:10-12 *(Today's New International Version)*

God owns everything—*everything* belongs to Him. Not just your home, your car, your bank account, your investments, but also the not so obvious—your family and friends, your children and your spouse. He is entrusting us with these people and possessions. He's counting on us to make decisions as He would.

So, how are you doing as His steward or trustee?

Where would you place yourself on the line below?

O———O———O———O———O———O———O———O———O———O

I am the owner   God is the owner

Go ahead. Mark where you think you are.

If you view God as the owner, that's great. It's huge. It is a mindset switch you've already undergone. You'll be affirmed by Him throughout this study and you'll also grow closer to Him as you allow Him to ignite this life of generosity in you.

If you put yourself anywhere else on the line, you view *yourself* as part owner, then believe it or not, that's great, too. Because you now recognize that there's a gap between where you are and where God is calling you to be. And the rest of this study will help you make that move.

Sit for a moment in silence. Reflect on what you just read about ownership. Pray—and ask the Holy Spirit to touch you.

Then write down what you sense He's telling you. He might bring a picture or an image of someone to mind. It could be a feeling you have. What is the Holy Spirit telling you?

If you didn't get any sense of God speaking to you, you're not alone. Just continue to come before Him and sit . . . and ask. He *will* speak.

And now—get ready for an adventure you'll never forget!

WHY DOES GOD MAKE SUCH A BIG DEAL ABOUT GIVING?

This may seem odd to you, but it began when I saw a beautiful dining-room set that I really wanted. I had set money aside for it—I loved everything about it. It went perfectly with my dining room. The problem was that I already had a perfectly good dining-room set . . . it just wasn't this one—with this wood grain, this style. What I had always wanted . . .

I battled with this decision for a while until finally I just sat down and wrote a check out for the amount of the new one—and sent it to a charity we supported. As soon as I mailed it—you won't believe this—but all my desire for the new dining-room set just disappeared.

It completely vanished.

On top of that, as I reflected on the struggle I went through, I couldn't believe that I had even wrestled over this decision—I almost didn't know who that person was. Whatever grip it had on my heart, as soon as I mailed that check . . . it just broke.

(Board member of a nonprofit financial ministry)

That's exactly what this is—a battle for your heart. The God of the Universe is calling to you, reaching out to you. He knows that the last thing we let go of is our money and our possessions.

You can't worship two gods at once. Loving one god, you'll end up hating the other. Adoration of one feeds contempt for the other. You can't worship God and Money both.

Matthew 6:24 *(The Message)*

God knows that there's a fierce battle raging—that there's an assault on your heart and mind that's sometimes daily, hourly or by the minute.

Take a moment to reflect on . . . you—what are you battling?

Is there a pattern to it? Does it occur at a certain time or place?

God doesn't want to take "your" money or TV or car or whatever else you might've written down. He wants your heart. He's crazy about you. He wants you to have a love relationship with Him, the God of the Universe. He knows you can't do that if your heart is being pulled and tempted by money and greed.

He also knows that the antidote to this heart pull is—Giving. Once you begin to give, the desire for "stuff" fades and greed begins to lose its grip on your heart. Once you start to give, the tide changes in this battle. You're giving up control and now are *trusting Him.*

No matter where you're at in this battle, can you think of at least one "antidote" you can take, that is, one way that you can give, that will begin to release this pull on your heart?

And if so, when's the earliest that you can take it?

DAY 4

CAN GOD BE TRUSTED?

I had just finished seminary and was without a job. Don't get me wrong. I wasn't destitute. I had a part time job and I was temporarily rooming with a friend. I had cashed in my 401(k) to pay for schooling and now I had only $200 left to my name.

And God spoke to me. Not audibly . . . but it was Him. I had just come back from a church service—and I couldn't even tell you what the sermon was about! But the teacher challenged us to trust God with everything.

And then I heard Him. Give my last $200 away. Wipe my account out . . . completely.

I thought, "Really? All of it?" And then I thought, "It's only $200. It's not tens of thousands or even thousands of dollars. Why not?" So I did. No big deal.

But it was. God wasn't through.

A few weeks later, I walked in from getting the mail. My friend Lee from the U.K. had written to me—and she never writes to me. She said she and her husband Peter were with their prayer group when God spoke to them. He said He wanted them to pray for me, and they did, like crazy. She jokingly asked if I had been lifted ten feet out of my chair a few weeks ago.

Then a check fell out. She also heard God tell her to send me £100, which converted to, you guessed it. $200.

I didn't really need that $200. But that wasn't His point. He was giving me a graduate level course that He obviously didn't think I had yet taken: Trusting God 301.

(A 32-year-old in career transition)

This is how God works. He provides. He can prompt any one of His children worldwide into action. He can also change deadlines, get loans approved, sell a house. He wants us to know He can be trusted—that He will provide.

God is able to shower all kinds of blessings on you. (And that) in all things and at all times you will have everything you need.

2 Corinthians 9:8 (New International Reader's Version)

Giving can be a scary thing . . . it can sometimes feel like you're giving up everything you ever wanted. But that's what the enemy does . . . he tries to download fear and lies into our minds . . . like we're in a free fall with no one to catch us.

So you have a choice to make. Are you going to believe the enemy's lies or trust God's promises?

And if you're not sure . . . how about testing His trustworthiness with just a small first step? He's a big God. He can handle your unbelief.

So what's one small thing you can trust Him with?

And for those of you who have already ignited this life of generosity in your heart, what's your next step to fan it into a larger flame? (To give more? To sell a business? To move?)

No one has any idea what He has in mind for you, but He does . . . just ask Him. You know He's good for it.

DAY 5

CAN YOU BE TRUSTED?

Many of us have heard about some of the outlandish demands made by music celebrities in their contracts with concert promoters. One of the most notorious came from the rock band Van Halen. Each contract insisted that "a bowl of M&Ms be provided backstage, but with every single brown M&M removed." If the band arrived and saw that the bowl had any brown M&Ms in it, they were free to cancel the concert and receive full payment. Who knew a bunch of hard-rockers could be such divas?

But wait.

There was actually a good reason behind the clause. The absence of those M&Ms was a matter of life or death. In his book *The Checklist Manifesto*, author Atul Gawande quoted from lead singer David Lee Roth's memoir to share the story behind the M&Ms:

Roth explained that . . . "Van Halen was the first band to take huge productions into tertiary, third-level markets. We'd pull up with nine 18-wheeler trucks, full of gear, where the standard was three trucks, max. And there were many, many technical errors—whether it was the girders couldn't support the weight, or the flooring would sink in, or the doors weren't big enough to move the gear through. The contract rider read like a . . . Yellow Pages because there was so much equipment and so many human beings to make it function."

So just as a little test, buried somewhere in the middle of the rider, would be Article 126, the no-brown-M&Ms clause. "When I would walk backstage, if I saw a brown M&M in that bowl," [Roth] wrote, "Well, we'd line-check the entire production. Guaranteed you'd run into a problem."[1] The mistakes could be life-threatening. . . . In Colorado, the band found that the local promoters had failed to read the weight requirements and that the staging would have fallen through the arena floor.

---

[1]Atul Gawande, *The Checklist Manifesto* (New York: Metropolitan Books, 2009), p. 80.

It's funny how Van Halen's ridiculous-at-first-glance contract demand illustrates so well Luke 16:10-11:

> *Whoever can be trusted with very little can also be trusted with much,*
> *and whoever is dishonest with very little will also be dishonest with much.*
> *. . . If you have not been trustworthy in handling worldly wealth, who will*
> *trust you with true riches?*
>
> *(New International Version)*

So, all this business about money is not about money. It's about true riches, which are people. If He can trust us with "little" when it comes to money, then He will ultimately entrust us with "much" when it comes to people's lives and eternities.

When we begin to trust God by becoming *trustworthy,* He will begin to bring more and more people to us . . . to you, to me. We are His hands and feet in the world. This world that so badly needs His touch, His heart, His love.

In what ways have you been trustworthy?

How did that feel?

Are there any situations you are in—right now or that are coming up—where you can continue to grow in this area of trustworthiness?

DAY 6

BEFORE MOVING ON . . .

For years, the Koromojong tribe in Africa had oppressed the neighboring Sabini tribe. Their actions had earned them the name "raiders" from the locals, which in their language meant, "killers and stealers of anything valuable." Women and children had been killed senselessly. Entire families were displaced because their homes were burned down. Several generations before, the entire tribe sought refuge in a nearby mountainous terrain called Kapchorwa. There, as in the lowlands, fresh water was a rare and precious resource.

Many from the Sabini tribe had become disciples of Jesus Christ as a result of missionary efforts. As they grew in their faith, they began to seek the Lord regarding how to put an end to the years of conflict and fear. While meeting together, Pastor Godwin of the church in Kapchorwa challenged everyone with a simple question, "What would Christ do?"

The numbers of both tribes were increasing, so water was getting scarcer. After a short time, the Sabini tribe decided that they, with the support of Sisters Community Church from Oregon and All Nations Ministries, would freely give the warring Koromojong the gift of water.

Within days, a local well driller was contracted, the equipment loaded, and Pastor Godwin headed off to the Koromojong with a partner from All Nations Ministries and two military guards. "Not many people would even attempt to approach the Koromojong, let alone expect to be let inside, and once inside there would be no guarantee of ever leaving alive," said Paul Rawlins from Sisters Community Church.[1]

Through God's grace, after a short confrontation with Koromojong guards, Pastor Godwin was able to share the intent and so was allowed into the village with the equipment. Tension was high, yet the curiosity about the equipment and process seemed to stabilize the Koromojong.

Within one week, the drillers had nearly completed the well. Curiosity had spread throughout the village so both leaders and village members arrived for the initial pumping of the water. During this process, Pastor Godwin began to preach about the living water of Jesus Christ and that He was the reason they were there. He shared that, through Jesus, all debts could be forgiven and all

---

[1] Mike Yankoski and Danae Yankoski, *Zealous Love: A Guide to Social Justice* (Grand Rapids: Zondervan, 2009).

wounds healed between the tribes. The words penetrated the hearts of the Koro-mojong tribe because they knew how their ancestors had treated the Sabini and how they themselves had continued this evil behavior. Soon, the well brought forth fresh water and cries of joy were heard from those present.

It also brought 600 warriors to their knees. They gave their lives to Christ that day.

That's what this is all about. And that's what it's ultimately about for you. Do you know Jesus as your Savior? As your best friend? In Day 3 we mentioned that this money issue is more about being in a relationship with our Creator . . . not about how we spend it. (He owns it all anyway, remember?)

> God saved you by his grace when you believed. And you can't take credit
> for this; it is a gift from God. Salvation is not a reward for the good
> things we have done, so none of us can boast about it.
>
> Ephesians 2:8-9 (New Living Translation)

We can't get to know Him more deeply, if we don't even know Him.

Take the president of the United States. Do you *know* him or do you know *of* him?

Most of us would have to say that we know *of* him and we know *about* him . . . but we don't really *know* him.

It's the same way with God. Do you really *know* Him or do you just know *of* Him? If it's the latter, the question you need to answer is what's keeping you from asking Him into your life to love and lead you?

If you'd like to do that, there are a few simple steps to take to insure that you are connected to God, that you receive this free gift of eternal life:

- **Admit you're a sinner.** Everyone has done things that displease a holy God. No one can live up to His standards. He says no sin can enter heaven. Something must be done to get rid of your sin. Romans 3:23 says, "All have sinned and fall short of the glory of God" (New International Version).

- **Believe Jesus died on the cross for you.** God loves you and wants you to become His child. He loves you so much that He sent His Son, Jesus, to shed His blood to save you from your sins. Jesus took your place on the cross and suffered the punishment you deserve. Believe that He died for you, was buried, and rose again on the third day. Acts 16:31 states, "Believe in the Lord Jesus, and you will be saved" (New International Version).

- **Call upon Jesus to save you.** Trust in Him as your Savior from sin. This may be a simple but sincere cry from your heart, or it may be expressed out loud. Romans 10:9 says, "If you confess with your mouth, 'Jesus is Lord,' and believe in your heart that God raised Him from the dead, you will be saved" (New International Version).

Jesus gave everything so that we may live, and His sacrifice was all-sufficient. A life of generosity flows from a love relationship with our Father and not from duty or rules. If you have any doubt where you stand, sit back down. He is waiting.

If you've never prayed . . .

Open: **Dear Father**

Admit: **I've sinned. I've done . . . (Name those sins that are weighing you down the most—you don't need to go through every one you've ever committed!)**

Believe: **I do believe that you sent your Son, Jesus, to die for my sins . . .**

Call: **Jesus, please come into my life, to save me and lead me.**

Thanks: **Thank you for coming into my life . . .**

You may or may not "feel" something. If you don't, don't worry. The fact is, if you meant it, then you are now His son or daughter! Congratulations!

Now go tell someone as soon as you can!

If you already have a relationship with Him, that's something to celebrate! Reflect on that and please pray for others working through this book that they come to know Him also.

Part Two

What Does He
Want You To Do?

DON'T STORE UP YOUR TREASURE ON EARTH

Over one million animal mummies have been found in Egypt, many of which are cats. It took 70 days to prepare each of them for burial!

Ancient Egyptians were buried with their belongings. The walls of their tombs were painted with scenes from the dead person's life. Tombs were also furnished with objects used during their life. These things were loaded into the tomb to accompany them to be used once they arrived in the afterlife. Furniture, weapons, games, food, all have been found . . . and of course pets, at least a million that we know of.

Archaeologists have uncovered the mummified cats, but hardly any jewels. Thieves aren't stupid—who's going to buy a dead cat?

Do not store up for yourselves treasures on earth, where moth and vermin destroy, and where thieves break in and steal. But store up for yourselves treasures in heaven, where moth and vermin do not destroy, and where thieves do not break in and steal. For where your treasure is, there your heart will be also.

Matthew 6:19-21 (New International Version)

Matthew clearly warns us about "storing up our treasures on earth." The question is, what's our treasure? The obvious answer is our money. The not-so-obvious answer for many of us is not only our money, but also *our time.*

So, the question we need to begin asking ourselves is where are we storing our treasure . . . where—exactly—are we spending our time and our money?

Reflect on that question. And if you have your schedule handy, look at it. (If you don't have it, think through your last five days.)

Where have you spent most of your time?
- Sleeping?
- Eating?
- Working?
- Being with your family?
- Being with your friends?
- Going to church?
- Volunteering?

How do you *feel* about where it's going?

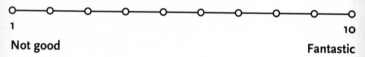

1   10
Not good   Fantastic

Reflect on your responses above.

DAY 8

DO STORE UP YOUR TREASURE IN HEAVEN

She came into our small group with red swollen eyes. She had been fired. We all knew that her supervisor had been gunning for her. And it finally happened. We listened to the whole sad, frustrating story. It was a nonprofit organization with no unemployment. So now she couldn't keep the apartment.

But what surprised me was what happened next. One of the husbands in the group was an HR professional. He immediately offered to help her with her resume and made an appointment with her, right there.

Another woman offered a room in her house—and meant it.

Later another person asked privately if we wanted to contribute some money for her.

And another small group member surprised her with a new suit for an interview (the HR professional also had gotten her an interview).

I had never seen anything like this in my life. I remember thinking, "Boy, they really take this community stuff seriously."

(A new church member)

> *Tell them to **use their money to do good**. They should be **rich in good works** and **generous to those in need**, always being **ready to share with others** [bolding added for emphasis]. By doing this they will be storing up their treasure as a good foundation for the future so that they may experience true life.*
>
> 1 Timothy 6:18-19 *(New Living Translation)*

This is God's New Community in action—Day 1 of this book. In Acts 2:42-47, they shared with those who were in need. And they actually sold possessions to help others out.

You, too, have done this. Think about your life, your actions. How have you "used your money to do good?" Because you have. Think back.

How have you been *rich in good works* (how have you used—or volunteered—your time to help others?)

How have you been *generous to those in need* (someone in your neighborhood or small group, someone who was homeless, poor, in jail)?

How have you been *ready to share with others* (shared or given clothes, meals, furniture)?

Please note: Everyone has given something to someone! So this journey we're on is about continuing to take small steps. It's not about what we haven't done, it's about what we can still do.

For those of you just starting out, what's a next step—a way that you can share or give of your time or money—that you think you can actually take?

For those of you who see yourself more toward the right side of the continuum—you've already started the generosity adventure. Reflect on all the lives He has touched through you, and thank God for being a Kingdom player!

So now the question is, what's the next step in this adventure? Is God prompting you to do something different?

Is He asking you to share your car? A room in your house? For a season? For a day? To give an investment? Sell some stock (even if you don't get the tax credit)?

Take a moment . . . quiet down. Let Him connect with you, with no guilt attached. What's the next step He has in store for *you*?

NOTICE THE OBVIOUS

I'm honeymooning with my bride and we're on a sailing ship in the Virgin Islands. We stop in a natural harbor and grab snorkeling gear to explore some incredible wildlife beneath the ocean.

We're in about six feet of water and I am stunned by the vision below me. I've never seen anything like it, never heard of it either—and I grew up in Southern California hitting the beach at every opportunity.

I pop up and call to Wendy to look down, and she does, but sees nothing.

"Look at the sea bed, everywhere!" I yell, energy and excitement adding power to my voice.

Head down, head up, head shaking. She doesn't see it.

"Squid!" I tell her, "baby squid, everywhere!"

Now she sees. The sea bed is layered with thousands of baby squid.

Every time we move, the squid rotate to watch us, little black eyes facing our human bodies.

The vision of those beautiful, transparent creatures travels with me whenever I visit the ocean. Amazing moments.

Back on the boat, Wendy told me that she didn't see the animals because they blended in with the sand at the bottom of the ocean. So they were invisible to her.

(Newlywed husband)

How often do we miss the obvious in our lives?

Unfortunately, many of us have to answer, "All too often." Many times we fail to see how God blesses us each day. When we reflect for just a moment on these things and acknowledge them, it becomes obvious that God has blessed us and that He cares deeply about us and is involved in our day-to-day lives.

We begin to remember and thank God for those obvious things that we may have overlooked in the past.

Having our hearts filled with gratitude allows us to joyfully give back to God.

Many, O LORD my God, are the wonders which You have done,
And Your thoughts toward us;
There is none to compare with You.
If I would declare and speak of them,
They would be too numerous to count.

Psalm 40:5 (New American Standard Bible)

Taking inventory of God's blessings is the first step to not missing the obvious and gaining a greater appreciation for His love.

Think about how you've been blessed by God. Use the space below to begin a list of all those "obvious" workings of God. Then read them through and talk to God about them.

If you need some help, you can use these categories:

- **How does the sacrifice of Jesus Christ impact your life?**

- **What spiritual blessings have you seen God provide?**

- **How has God blessed your health?**

- **How has God provided each day for you and your family?**

- **What friendships has He blessed you with?**

- **How were you blessed from a recent mission experience or outreach event?**

DAY 10

DRIVE YOUR STAKE
INTO THE GROUND

Each year Americans spend

$2 billion on cosmetics
$5 billion on perfumes and colognes
$20 billion on ice cream
$40 billion on lawn care

And $450 billion is what we spend each year at Christmas.

Do you know it would take just $20 billion to meet the food needs of
the whole world?
So when do we have enough? When do we have too much?

> Not that I was ever in need, for **I have learned how to be content with
> whatever I have** [bolding added for emphasis]. I know how to live on
> almost nothing or with everything. I have learned the secret of living in
> every situation, whether it is with a full stomach or empty, with plenty
> or little.
>
> Philippians 4:11-12 (New Living Translation)

Paul learned contentment—contentment with what he had, not with
what he didn't have.
There are many competing voices offering us gratification from many
different places. They are saying that the more we have, the better off we'll
be. This might be the devil's favorite lie—that satisfaction in life comes
from our own "collection of islands."
It's time to drive a stake in the ground.
It's time to say, "That's enough."

It's time to recognize that neither what we have nor what we want is ours. None of it belongs to us.

It is all our Creator's and He would prefer that instead of gathering, we were giving; giving and sharing with people on this planet who have so much less than we do.

Do you really need another eyeliner, another ice cream cone, or greener grass?

How are you doing? What's your "enough?"

Take a moment. Reflect . . .

○ On your house. Is the size *enough* for you? Has it had enough improvements?

○ Your clothes. Are there *enough* in your closet?

○ Electronics. Do you need the latest technology or is your current phone or TV or computer enough?

○ Or something else?

We all have an area where we tend to spend more than we need to. What's yours? Check the one above.

Then quantify it. Put a dollar amount on it . . . how much would you save if you didn't spend any more or spent a lot less? What would that amount be?

What could you do with that money? What Kingdom impact could it have? Stop and pray . . . right now. Ask God what He wants you to do.

You may get a thought or an impression. If you do, write it down below. Act on it, whatever it is. Then—watch out for what God might do with that impulse.

DAY 11

HAVE A PLAN

Jim was brought in to help a large Christian school facing its 16th year of financial struggles. After the president shared his frustration, Jim finally asked, "Have you ever put a plan in place to change this pattern?" At first, the president was a little defensive, and then he was embarrassed. Finally, he just put Jim in charge of the financial plan.

(A seasoned mentor)

How about you? Are you regularly facing too much month and not enough pay to give faithfully?

You might even be feeling a little overwhelmed at this point. You're feeling like you want to begin giving or begin giving more, but you don't know how to go about it . . . and you might even be feeling a little guilty. Stop.

Remember, this isn't about the money. It's about your relationship with the Giver. He wants to invite you into an adventure with Him. One that's dependent upon Him and Him alone. So, begin by leaning into Proverbs 21:5:

Careful planning puts you ahead in the long run; hurry and scurry puts you further behind.

(The Message)

Begin with a simple plan. That plan should include giving, saving and providing.

Giving: Giving in the New Testament (2 Corinthians 8:12) is according to your means, and acceptable giving is linked to what you have. Develop a plan that moves you towards giving according to your ability. Over time take steps to give sacrificially.

Saving: Proverbs 21:20 says, "The wise store up choice food and olive oil, but fools gulp theirs down" (New International Version). The Bible consistently refers to saving for future emergency needs, like the loss of a job or unexpected bills. However, as disciples we are called to live by faith

(2 Corinthians 5:7) and have a clear warning in Luke 12 to not depend on money or on our own abilities, but to completely trust God for provision.

You have what's left over to provide for your family. First Timothy 5:8 says it strongly:

> *But those who won't care for their relatives, especially those in their own household, have denied the true faith. Such people are worse than unbelievers.*
>
> *(New Living Translation)*

At this point, we have to discuss debt. You use money out of the "providing" category to begin paying off debt. Obtaining a solid biblical debt reduction resource or advisor can walk you through how to begin wiping out your debt—all of it—so that you're on your way to financial freedom. When you're debt free, you've freed up God's resources to be used however He directs.

Here are some basic steps to consider:

1. **Set goals.** These goals should be both short term (six months) and long term (two to three years) and include specifics about giving, debt reduction and planned expenses.

2. **Develop a budget.** A budget is the basic framework for a good financial plan. Typically, giving decisions are determined after all of the income and expenses are listed, but God's Word states that this should be deducted first from our income. A good resource to develop a basic budget that includes giving can be found through Crown Financial Ministries or Good Sense Ministries.

3. **Put the plan into action.** Follow-through is a common struggle in budgeting or giving. Develop a budget; then be purposeful about putting the plan into action. Do it immediately. Waiting will diffuse the success of any plan and often results in the plan fizzling out.

4. **Stay accountable to the plan.** Track income, giving and expenses using a basic spreadsheet. Review biweekly or monthly to compare how reality aligns with your plans. This exercise will allow you to make adjust-

ments where necessary and stay on target. Your ability to give consistently to your church or other organizations will help them to better forecast to plan ministry. Another discipline that helps families stay accountable is an envelope system. When families withdraw planned giving or expenses immediately after being paid and put those amounts into envelopes, they become a strong visual reminder to stay on track.

The latter part of Proverbs 21:5 cautions us that a hurried approach to financial management will be riddled with thoughtless actions. Impulse buying quickly leads to poverty. It is a pattern of spending that will drastically reduce the amount that can be given towards God's work.

Each day, there will be many temptations or circumstances that will distract you from your plan. But God promises, in Proverbs 16:3, that if you "Put God in charge of your work, then what you've planned will take place" (The Message).

You've just read through a lot of information. Take a moment to think through what your next step is (putting a budget together, getting out of debt, deciding on an overall plan, getting help, etc.).

Next step:

By when:

Now, stop and pray over this decision—pray that God will go before you and provide for you as you carry out this plan.

BEGIN GIVING

Picture yourself on this journey.

You're in ancient Israel at a grand festival. Friends and family members surround you. On everyone's shoulders are beautiful baskets, some crafted of gold and silver, others woven from willow branches.

Live birds are tied to the baskets, adding a little chaos of fluttering wings and sound to the joy and fun as you walk toward the Temple in Jerusalem.

There you are greeted by flutists. Their song directs you further on your journey to the Temple Mount where priests join you and begin to sing.

The birds are then offered as sacrifices and you recite the traditional declaration which is part of hundreds of years of tradition:

> *My father was a wandering Aramean, and he went down into Egypt with a few people and lived there and became a great nation, powerful and numerous. But the Egyptians mistreated us and made us suffer, putting us to hard labor. Then we cried out to the LORD, the God of our ancestors, and the LORD heard our voice and saw our misery, toil and oppression. So the LORD brought us out of Egypt with a mighty hand and an outstretched arm, with great terror and with miraculous signs and wonders. He brought us to this place and gave us this land, a land flowing with milk and honey; and now I bring the first fruits of the soil that you, LORD, have given me.*
>
> Deuteronomy 26:5-10 *(New International Version)*

You have just offered your Bikkurim, your first fruits to God. You are following Proverbs 3:9.

> *Honor the LORD with your wealth, with the first fruits of all your crops.*
>
> *(New International Version)*

You are giving your first fruits to Him, to His temple. Or nowadays, to His Church, to those who minister to us.

And since God knows that can be emotionally scary for us, He actually tells us to test Him. To *trust* Him. And if we do that, He will then deliver this promise.

> *Bring the whole tithe into the storehouse, that there may be food in my house. Test me in this," says the Lord Almighty, "and see if I will not throw open the floodgates of heaven and pour out so much blessing that there will not be enough room to store it.*
>
> *Malachi 3:10 (New International Version)*

In the Old Testament they were to give 10% to God (Leviticus 27:30-33), 10% for the festivals and 10% every third year for the Levites and the poor who had no portion of land (Deuteronomy 14:22-29). In the New Testament, Jesus emphasizes giving according to your ability and to grow as a sacrificial giver. If you're at a place where you are not giving . . . *then give something*. Test Him. See what He does.

And then, as you are able, increase your giving so that you're giving sacrificially.

However, Jesus doesn't stop there. Remember ALL of what we have is His. So as He prompts, learn to drive your stake into the ground and to say, "Enough is enough. Anything I make beyond this amount goes toward His work and those in need." So you may end up giving more proportionately than you ever imagined. Unbelievable!

Imagine . . . what "God-things" could happen with that money? What child or family could you help? What town or village could you help with fresh water? What micro-business could you support, so that a mom or dad could buy a uniform for their child to go to school? What house could you help fix up or build for that single mom who is homeless?

It begins with the "first fruits." Making "giving to God and His word" our first commitment.

A recent survey reported that on average individuals only give three percent of their income.[1]

Giving our first fruits, according to our means, and sacrificially, begins when our actions align with our beliefs about God. The physical act of giving *first* to the Lord puts our faith into action. It demonstrates that we believe He is our first priority.

So, where are you on your journey to the Temple? How much are you giving to the things of God?

How much are you being prompted to give?

---

[1] Survey by Barna Research Group, 2007. www.barna.org/barna-update/congregations/41 -new-study-shows-trends-in-tithing-and-donating#.VH4mccmtYXw.

DAY 13

BEGIN GIVING . . . SACRIFICIALLY

In the late 1800s, a young girl named Hattie May Wiatt attended a very small Pennsylvania church, which was regularly overcrowded. She heard that future plans included building a larger church and Sunday school room.

Sometime after learning this, she got very sick and died. After her funeral, her mother brought 57 cents to the pastor of their church. Hattie May Wiatt had been saving this money as her contribution toward a larger facility that could hold more children. The pastor took the gift and had it changed into pennies. Then he took the pennies to the members of the church and stated that they had received their first contribution toward a larger facility. He offered the 57 pennies for sale.

The 57 pennies sold for a total of about $250.

The pastor then took the $250 and changed all of it into pennies and offered them for sale as well. From the sale of these pennies, he received enough to buy the house next door.

This initial gift of 57 cents led to the formation of the Wiatt Mite Society, the purpose of which was to enlarge upon the first 57 cents given by Hattie May Wiatt. Using the influence of this little child's gift, the Society raised additional funds and the congregation continued to grow. By 1912, this church had grown to over 5,600 members.

It was in this same church that several institutions were founded. These institutions include Samaritan Hospital, now called Temple University Hospital, which has helped cure and minister to thousands, as well as Temple University, which has educated more than 80,000 young people.

(A young director of development)

The thought of such an eternal impact is almost mind-boggling. It's beyond our comprehension. God used a little girl with a sacrificial heart to accomplish great things through a simple act of faith.

And He looked up and saw the rich putting their gifts into the treasury. And He saw a poor widow putting in two small copper coins. And He said, "Truly I say to you, this poor widow put in more than all of them;

*for they all out of their surplus put into the offering; but she out of her
poverty put in all that she had to live on.*

Luke 21:1-4 (New American Standard Bible)

A careful examination of Jesus' words in Luke 21 reveals that God's
standard of generosity is radically different than the world's. In fact, the
one who gave the least amount of money actually gave the most in the
Lord's eyes! What was it about this giving transaction that honored God
so much? It wasn't because she carefully considered the impact her gift
would have, nor that she was noticed by others. And it's clear that it wasn't
the amount of her gift.

In verse 3, Jesus shares the secret: she *sacrificed*. She gave out of her
poverty. There are two key observations we can make. One, she was willing
to part with all that she had for God's glory, and two, she trusted that God
would provide for *all* her future needs.

The Greek word for poverty in verse 3 is *ptōchos*, the same word used
for "poor." Words like needy, destitute, lacking, and without means all
capture the heart of what Jesus is trying to communicate here. Materially,
this widow was clearly poor, but we can also see that she was "poor in
spirit," which is a reflection of her heart as she made the gift. She realized
she was lacking in every way and that only God could provide what she
needed both materially and spiritually.

As a result, she gave sacrificially out of her love for God. Rather than
giving from a sense of duty or obligation, she trusted Him to provide for
her future needs. It's this kind of giving that honors God most.

> **The most humbling words are in verse one: "He saw." He was
> watching. He is still watching. If you've never considered this truth
> before as you make pledge commitments or as you give to support
> God's work, how would it make a difference in how you give?**

DAY 14

GIVE FAITHFULLY

My prayer partner from graduate school told me that God was leading her to send me a check each month for six months. I was thrilled. But I also knew that Teri didn't have any money.

I was doing a non-paid internship in the Netherlands and really did need money badly. And then she told me the amount—twenty dollars each month . . . for six months.

What? Was that all? I couldn't believe it. I wanted to tell her, "Keep your money; this isn't going to help me with anything." But I couldn't. What do you say to someone who says "God is leading me" except "OK, thanks."

So I received the first two checks and felt silly cashing them—like this was a ridiculous exercise. But they kept coming.

It started with the fourth check.

I began to change.

I began to connect with my Father in a way I'd never done before. I was humbled by her faithfulness. She wasn't even embarrassed by the size of the checks. Ever.

God asked her to send checks for six months, so she did. No questions, she just obeyed. We both knew it wasn't going to make a dent in anything. But she did it anyway. And the lesson was mine. I began to feel God's unwavering love for me. His concern. His faithfulness through that tangible check each month. Through her faithfulness, He taught me faithfulness.

Then Teri's story became mine.

God used that object lesson to model for me what He wanted to do through my life. When I returned home, He had me pick up where she left off.

First, He prompted me to give a few hundred dollars to a friend of mine for six months—every month for six months. That was hard. And it surprised me that it was hard. I realized that it was much easier for me to just write one check and be done with it. But to be in someone's life for that period of time, well, that was a different story. So after the third month, I was beginning to feel that maybe I had given enough. But I remembered Teri—who was faithful with little. If she could do it, I could do it. I needed to be faithful. And I was. It was a huge accomplishment, me and God taking care of one of His kids.

The next six months of giving was to a man who volunteered at our church. He loved serving in the toddler area and faithfully served our three kids. He was injured and lost his job in the process. God prompted me again. Again it was for six months, but this time it was to give a much larger amount. My husband and I did. Another adventure. Another life impacted by His faithfulness—another son that the Father wanted to remind that He was there, that He cared and that He would provide.

The journey continues. We never know when and who God is going to ask us to give His money to. But we have it ready.

(A working mom)

In Matthew 25:21, the Master praises His servant,

Well done, good and faithful servant! You have been faithful with a few things; I will put you in charge of many things. Come and share your master's happiness!

(New International Version)

Aren't those words the ones that you long to hear?

How have you already been faithful with God in the past—or present? Write down those things that come to mind.

When you think of wanting to become more faithful, what is one thing you believe God is nudging you about?

Is anything holding you back from becoming more faithful? If it's becoming more faithful at giving, is it because you're worried about providing for yourself or your family?

Jesus said, "The thief comes only to steal and kill and destroy" (John 10:10, New American Standard Bible). Part of the enemy's strategy is provoking fear about your future and whether you will have all that you will need. In the second part of that verse, Jesus goes on to state, "I came that they may have life, and have it abundantly."

Dare to trust God. Dare to be faithful.

Go back and read what you just wrote about wanting to become more faithful. What's one step you think you can take to help you do that?

DAY 15

GIVE QUIETLY

He wears a $15 watch and doesn't own a house or a car. Few people would ever suspect that Chuck Feeney has discretely donated more than $4 billion through a charitable organization he founded, by confidentially moving 100 percent of his stock into an off-shore company. He was so secretive that his own business partner was not aware of the legacy of generosity he would leave.

The story surfaced only when his firm, The Duty Free Shoppers' Group, was sold and the extent of his equity, $1.6 billion, became public.

This quiet giver, Chuck Feeney, and his organization gave several billion dollars to under-resourced people around the world. (Check out his charity at www.atlanticphilanthropies.org.) Chuck's charity operated on one main rule: that no one was ever to know his name.

(A humbled giver)

How does this idea of anonymity sit with you? With any of us? You'd think you should get some credit for giving. After all, you need a receipt for tax purposes. And you'd think that Feeney could, by going public about his enormous contributions, inspire others to give generously as well.

However, Jesus gives a stern warning against giving in order to be noticed by others. In fact, He clearly states that there is no eternal reward for this type of giving.

Beware of practicing your righteousness before men to be noticed by them; otherwise you have no reward with your Father who is in heaven. So when you give to the poor, do not sound a trumpet before you, as the hypocrites do in the synagogues and in the streets, so that they may be honored by men. Truly I say to you, they have their reward in full. But when you give to the poor, do not let your left hand know what your right hand is doing, so that your giving will be in secret; and your Father who sees what is done in secret will reward you.

Matthew 6:1-4 (New American Standard Bible)

Jesus' concern isn't so much about men observing our giving as much as it's about our heart being in the proper condition when we give. Our giving should be an affair of the heart with God, a natural outflow of our love for Him.

Giving quietly is a way to grow more intimate with our Creator because it communicates that we're really only concerned with pleasing Him and not with pleasing others. If Christ is our highest priority in life, then the fact that He notices will be more than enough.

Take some time right now to just pray—to sit before God and ask Him to touch your heart. To bring peace . . . and quiet.

Prayer:
"Lord, I want to please you and not other people. Help me to quiet those voices that urge me to want attention, or to get credit for an idea or business deal. Please help me have pure motives. Please quiet my soul."

GIVE PRAYERFULLY

You could hear a pin drop. The ministry's chief financial officer just shared their projected financial troubles. He pointed out that the ministry needed $38,000 in two weeks to meet expenses.

After hearing his report, the leadership team knew that it was going to be a challenging week. They spent the morning in prayer. Afterwards, the development director got in his car and headed toward his next appointment.

He was prompted by the Lord to begin making calls to close friends. The first call resulted in confirmation of a $13,000 gift. He attended his meeting and shortly after, made another call which resulted in an immediate gift of $3,000. When he returned to the office, he had received an email from a friend who shared about the work God was doing in his life—how he had been praying about an amount to give and that he had received confirmation to put a check in the mail for $25,000.

As the development director looked at the timing of his email, he realized that his response was sent about one hour after the leadership team finished praying that morning. In just under four hours, God provided $41,000.

(A ministry staff member)

The common focus for both the ministry and the givers involved was God. As they sought His will, He used prayer to orchestrate a divine plan of blessing and provision. This modern-day story is proof that God still hears and answers the prayers of His people when they diligently seek Him. He guides His people who seek to know where and how much to give, and He guides ministries that seek where to find it and how to discover it.

As you consider decisions such as how much to give, where to give, and when to give, seek the Lord for His guidance. His promise is to guide us when we pray, and we can trust He is orchestrating a divine appointment to provide for His perfect plan.

It's sad how sometimes we are so foolish to worry, forgetting God has His hand on us all.

Be anxious for nothing, but in everything by prayer and supplication
with thanksgiving let your requests be made known to God.

Philippians 4:6 (New American Standard Bible)

Are you aware of any needs? Is God calling you to be His hands and feet and to contribute your time, talents or treasures to help meet those needs? Perhaps you are eager to be a blessing and have just held back. Prayer is fundamental to determining your next step.

Spend some time in prayer right now. Listen for God's still, small voice. How is He speaking to you?

If you find it helpful, use this space to write down your prayers.

DAY 17

GIVE GENEROUSLY
(AKA: Do I Give on the Net or the Gross?)

We had a blast this past Christmas. The highlight was when our entire family decided we were going to give money away to people who were a part of a micro-loan organization. You lend someone money, they pay you back and then you can reinvest it with another person. We got so caught up in it that we spent almost two hours looking through people's profiles and what they needed a loan for.

Each of our kids (10, 10 and 12 years old) gathered around our laptop and began looking at the different businesses people wanted to start. The girls decided to lend money to several different people—mainly women, mainly moms trying to get their kids books or a tin roof instead of a cardboard one. They got so caught up in it they pleaded with us to let them give away the entire $50 check they each received from their aunt—and then they did!

My son approached it differently. He had an amount he planned to give and stuck to it. My husband and I had just realized that we were at the end of the year and we "owed" God! We give to our church, but then above that we give to other nonprofits. So we had more to give to His work! My husband and I had wanted to give for a while, and this was our chance! As I said, we all had a blast! And we still laugh about one person we tried to loan money to, but someone else beat us to it! Being the competitive family we are, we clearly "lost!"

It was an incredible feeling to see our kids completely caught up in this giving experience . . . it was an incredible feeling for us to be completely caught up in it.

(A wife and mom)

Remember this—a farmer who plants only a few seeds will get a small crop. But the one who plants generously will get a generous crop. You must each decide in your heart how much to give. And don't give reluctantly or in response to pressure. "For God loves a person who gives cheerfully."

2 Corinthians 9:6-7 (New Living Translation)

You may have heard this concept—you reap what you sow. This is the scripture passage it comes from. Paul is telling us that if our heart is stingy, and we only want to give a little, then we'll reap a measly crop. He's not going to tell us whether to tithe on the net or the gross. What he does tell us, however, is that if we want to "reap lavishly" then we need to sow lavishly.

So you need to decide—in your heart—what you want to reap: a small crop or a huge one. And remember, it's not the size of the gift—it never has been. It's about the size of our heart. So the litmus test is whether we're giving cheerfully or reluctantly ("I want to give away the least amount possible.") If it's the latter, then that's a clue that our heart isn't right . . . yet.

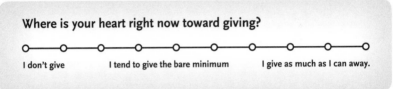

Where is your heart right now toward giving?

I don't give   I tend to give the bare minimum   I give as much as I can away.

Wherever you are is fine. If you're on the right-hand side, you need to celebrate and thank God for the transformation He has brought in your life!

If you're more to the left, like most of us, then you still need inner change to experience the cheerful giving that God desires for our life. The Greek word for cheerful is *hilaros*, which is where we derive the word hilarious. God wants hilarious givers.

Think about it.

If you're filled with joy, so much so that you find it "hilarious," how generous do you think you'll end up being? What if we could all be that way about giving—all the time? What would your world look like? What would *our world* look like?

Only Jesus can transform our hearts to be this way. But many times it begins with us taking a step of faith . . . and then He meets us as we step out.

As always, the choice is ours.

How is He asking you to step out?

Stop. Pray that Jesus would help you take this step and bring about this inner change in you.

Part Three

Ignite the Fire!

THE ADVENTURE
OF A LIFETIME

A few years ago, a best-selling book captured the attention and imagination of the country.

One Hundred Things to Do Before You Die inspired people young and old to create their bucket lists. Desires ranged from simple to imaginative to impossible. Authors Freeman and Teplica observe that "This life is a short journey."[1] So you'd better make some memories before you go.

What would your adventure, from a few events on their list, include?

- Iditarod Sled Dog Race in Alaska
- Cannes Film Festival in France
- Oktoberfest in Germany
- Running of the Bulls in Spain
- Yom Kippur at Israel's Western Wall

Or would your desires be more modest or more local?

- Invent a board game
- Build your dream home
- Do standup comedy

There is one adventure God wants you to experience . . .

*Since you excel in so many ways—in your faith, your gifted speakers, your knowledge, your enthusiasm, and your love from us—**I want you to excel also in this gracious act of giving** [bolding added for emphasis]. . . . And God will generously provide all you need. Then you will always have everything you need and plenty left over to share with others.*

---

[1] Dave Freeman and Neil Teplica, *100 Things To Do Before You Die* (Lanham, MD: Taylor Trade Publishers, 1999), p. 8.

As the Scriptures say,

> *"They share freely and give generously to the poor.*
> *Their good deeds will be remembered forever."*
>
> 2 *Corinthians 8:7; 9:8-9 (New Living Translation)*

Your deeds will be remembered forever. Really? Isn't that an exaggeration?

But that's what God says. This will be a short devotional today. Just one question for you.

How do you envision your life if you excelled in this act of giving?

YOUR KINGDOM ASSIGNMENT

Pastor Andy Stanley of North Point Community Church asks the question, "What do you need to live on?"

Then he answers it with a simple statement:

"You need food, shelter and a vehicle to get to work. ALL ELSE IS EXTRA."

ALL ELSE IS EXTRA.

Extra shirts, shoes, stuff, things—all of it is EXTRA.

What do you really need? What can you share?

Will you give to Kingdom purposes, save some, and live on the rest?

Learn to live without the EXTRA.

Each of us needs to answer that question. And our answer to that question is critical.

(A downsizing Christ follower)

So then each one of us will give an account of himself to God.

Romans 14:12 (New American Standard Bible)

Imagine the day when you will stand before the Most High God for the most important question ever. Doesn't the thought of standing face-to-face before the Creator, who knows our every thought and action, bring an overwhelming sense of humility and reverent fear? Just thinking of that moment creates a healthy sense of urgency and purpose that often seems missing in our daily lives.

Romans tells us that we will all give an account of our lives, implying that each of us has been entrusted by God with a unique amount of time, talent, and treasure that we will answer for. We have the awesome privilege to serve as stewards of our King's possessions.

Is that healthy sense of urgency missing in your everyday life?

How has the busyness of life distracted you from what really matters?

If you were told that the Lord would take you home next month, what might your management of God's resources look like? Would it be different than on every other day in your life? Should it be?

On that day, as we stand before almighty God, all that will matter about our earthly possessions is how they were used for Him. What was accomplished for eternity?

Ask God to search deep within you concerning how you handle possessions.

Ask Him to reveal areas you have never submitted to Him.

Acknowledge your desire to prepare for that day of account.

MORE WILL BE ENTRUSTED TO YOU

John Beckett was a successful businessman from the Midwest. He faced a huge challenge. He and a few other businessmen were positioned to purchase land projected to be a very lucrative investment. During this time, John and his wife were approached by Dr. Bill Bright, president of Campus Crusade for Christ. He shared with them an opportunity to help a Christian college in New York facing tremendous financial challenges. The need was large and if they chose to help the college, it would mean sacrificing the investment property. Only God could direct the outcome.

While praying over a decision, they learned of an elderly woman who gave sacrificially to help that college. Her act of generosity touched them deeply. It appeared the Lord had used her story to confirm their decision. John and his wife obeyed God's leading and gave the college all they had set aside for the real estate investment. God used the vision of Dr. Bright and the testimony of an elderly woman who gave sacrificially to propel them in a completely different direction.

Now John and his wife can see how their decision helped thousands of young students be trained for Christian leadership. This couple is a modern example of ten-talent stewards. Rather than real estate, their investment will multiply through the lives of these students and have an incomprehensible impact for the Kingdom.

(A Christian who wants to leave a legacy)

He called his servants together and delegated responsibilities. To one he gave five thousand dollars, to another two thousand, to a third one thousand, depending on their abilities. Then he left. Right off, the first servant went to work and doubled his master's investment. The second did the same. But the man with the single thousand dug a hole and carefully buried his master's money.

After a long absence, the master of those three servants came back and settled up with them. The one given five thousand dollars showed him how he had doubled his investment. His master commended him: "Good work! You did your job well. From now on be my partner."

The servant with the two thousand showed how he also had doubled

his master's investment. His master commended him: "Good work! You
did your job well. From now on be my partner."

Matthew 25:14-23 *(The Message)*

We must approach each day with the same wisdom and courage as the servant in Matthew 25 who returned the ten talents for the five. His approach was to trade that which was of lesser value for something of greater value. This would require "releasing" what he had for that which was of greater value in the eyes of his Master.

Giving resources entrusted to us for the advancement of God's kingdom and glory is fundamental to this principle. On Days 7 and 8, we looked at Matthew 6:19 where Jesus says, "Do not store up for yourselves treasures on earth, where moth and vermin destroy, and where thieves break in and steal" (New International Version).

We're to focus our investments into eternal treasures that last and multiply. How wonderful it will be to meet the faces of those who were reached for Christ, or those who grew closer to Him, as a result of our investment and generosity towards His work.

Regardless of how much you have, you can be a ten-talent steward. But for this to happen, we must be intentional and live purposefully, to be a tool for advancing God's Kingdom on earth. It may be a small gift, a meeting with a friend, or a skill you have that can be offered to a local ministry. Whatever it is, you will be amazed at how quickly your investment multiplies when God is involved.

So, as you think about John and his wife and the faithful servant in Jesus' parable—how have you seen God work that way in your life?

> **Think back. What have you given in time or money that you saw God use to impact someone's life—or maybe multiple lives?**

Celebrate. Thank God for what He has done in your life and through your life. And as you go into this next phase of this adventure, think strategically, act with purpose, and leave the rest to God!

WHAT ARE WE HERE FOR?

The family is on vacation, visiting my wife's folks in St. Louis, and Josh, my seven-year-old, runs crying into the house. Below his right eye, there's a bizarre lump and a knot sticks out. It's gruesome. He's sobbing and making all these crying noises, which means without an interpreter we have no clue what happened.

Rebekah, our youngest, comes in to translate. "Josh climbed a tree and fell out. He climbed a tree higher than the top of the house."

"Show me the tree." My wife holds Josh while I'm led to the backyard. Bekah points to a tree towering above the roof. At the base bricks are laid into the ground.

"Josh fell and landed on his head. His hands were at his sides and he just flew straight down and landed on his head."

How can this boy be standing in the living room crying on my wife's shoulder?

Now I'm scared, so we drive to the hospital.

The doctor tests his neck, shoulders, spine—all the things that should have broken from this kind of fall. And every fifteen seconds or so, she glances up at me with this funny look on her face.

"He fell how far?"

I say, "Eighteen to twenty feet."

"Landed on his head?"

"Right," I tell her. "That's the lump below his eye." It is already disappearing.

"Let's get his head X-rayed."

Our doctor is baffled by the lack of injury. The X-ray of his skull is a hundred percent normal, and they give Josh his own big black photograph of that invincible head. It hangs above his bed today.

As my wife and I sit at his side, I begin fighting tears. "He should be dead or at least have a broken neck." She's tearing up as well, shaking her head, not wanting to think those thoughts.

We drive back to her parents' home and all we could talk about was this . . .

Why is he still here? Why is Josh still alive?

(A husband and dad)

So here's the big takeaway—a question:

What are you here for?

We believe our lives are meant to touch others. To connect and contribute to the earthly—and eternal—experience of everyone we encounter.

The family in the story has a mission statement. It can apply to anything, but is specific enough that you know when it's happening. They all use it, all three kids, the wife and the husband.

Their mission statement is: BE A BLESSING.

Leave people in a better place than you found them. Build them up.

There's basically only two ways to do that. Remember our treasures? We have our time and we have our money.

With our time, we can bless people through a wide range of experiences. It either can be more spontaneous, like when we connect relationally with people at basketball games or church, or with our family and extended family. It can also be more planned out, like when we help our neighbor, or when we volunteer at church or a local food pantry.

With our finances, we can also bless people in a number of different ways.

Imagine leveraging your giving for the maximum impact possible—being able to touch hundreds and thousands of people across the planet—but also being able to help your divorced neighbor—a single mom or dad—with groceries or a house payment.

Through our giving, we become the conduit whereby God blesses others.

> . . . In the same way, he will provide and increase your resources and then produce a great harvest of generosity in you. **Yes, you will be enriched in every way so that you can always be generous.** And when we take your gifts to those who need them, they will thank God. **So two good things will result from this ministry of giving—the needs of the believers . . . will be met, and they will joyfully express their thanks to God. . . . And they will pray for you with deep affection because of the overflowing grace God has given to you** [bolding added for emphasis].

> 2 Corinthians 9:10-14 (New Living Translation)

You can offer your time, talent and treasure.

Be a blessing.

What does that mean to you?

This is the last day of this devotional—spend some time with Him.

Where do you sense God wanting you to be a blessing? Pray as you go through this . . . what is God most impressing upon you?

Being a blessing in the life of:

money	time	
O	O	My spouse (ex-spouse)
O	O	My son/daughter
O	O	My mom/dad
O	O	My brother/sister
O	O	A friend
O	O	Someone I work with
O	O	Someone in my neighborhood/church/small group
O	O	Someone I see regularly (at the gas station/restaurant/park)

Being a blessing in:

money	time	
O	O	My church
O	O	A ministry in my church
O	O	An urban ministry
O	O	A ministry in another country

Now go back and write down how you want to be a blessing. For example, if you marked the time box next to "My spouse," you may want to spend a date night two times per month on Saturday night starting at 6:30 pm. Write that in the space provided and then let your spouse know (and find a sitter if needed!).

Or if you wanted to spend time with a ministry, write down when you're going to contact them, how many hours and which day(s) you can volunteer during the month, and when you can start. Start by listening to their needs and see if you have a talent or an ability that will help them better accomplish their mission.

You may want to give sacrificially to someone in need or a ministry. If you're married, let your spouse know and then figure out when and how you're going to give.

Or if you wanted to give money to someone in your small group, community or family, write down when you want to start, how much and for how long.

If you marked more than two, prioritize them and then just focus on the top one or two. Don't overwhelm yourself. This is critical. The enemy would be ecstatic if he can keep you from what you intend. And one of his main tactics is to trick us into trying to do too much. Because he knows that if we try to do too much, we won't do anything at all.

This is it. This is the end of our time together. But this is just the beginning of your adventure with God—with Him not only igniting . . . but fanning the flames of generosity in your life.

Yes, you will be enriched in every way so that you can always be generous.
. . . And they will pray for you with deep affection because
of the overflowing grace God has given to you.

2 Corinthians 9:11, 14 (New Living Translation)

SMALL GROUP STUDY GUIDE

WEEK 1—LIVING AS EXILES

Acts 4:32-35: *All the believers were united in heart and mind. And they felt that what they owned was not their own, so they shared everything they had. The apostles testified powerfully to the resurrection of the Lord Jesus, and God's great blessing was upon them all. There were no needy people among them, because those who owned land or houses would sell them and bring the money to the apostles to give to those in need. (New Living Translation)*

Potlatch

"The great deeds." That's, roughly, how to translate *potlatch*, a Hul'qumi'num (*Hull*-cum-*me*-num) word. For Coast Salish people, the potlatch marked a great deed, a great happening—a victory, a wedding, a funeral, a birth. The potlatch was the party you threw, the banquet you held, the festival you hosted, to announce that something much bigger than yourselves had taken place. Something's happened, maybe by your own doing, maybe not, that defines those who are part of it in new ways. You are now a chief, or a husband, or a victor, or a father.

Only a potlatch can adequately mark the occasion.

At the heart of the potlatch was sheer bounty. It was preeminently about giving and receiving. It was sharing wealth in the most literal and extravagant way. Everything was up for grabs. No possession was so valuable it couldn't be vouchsafed to another. One's riches were measured by one's generosity. The more you gave, the wealthier you were. . . . The Canadian government condemned it and outlawed it. A culture that measured wealth on the scale of possessions could not grasp wealth measured on the scale of donations. Away with the heathen nonsense!

Of course, that heathen nonsense was closer to the heart of God than our materialism. It's not unlike the exchange of wealth described in Acts 2 and 4, where a Spirit-emboldened people can't give away their wealth to each other fast enough.[1]

As followers of Jesus, we are to live as exiles in this world. We are to stand out. We don't belong here, and we should act like it. Perhaps more than any other area of our lives, our material wealth poses the greatest opportunity to stand out to a watching world. But our material wealth may be our greatest stumbling block. In America, we have a culture that believes accumulation is our greatest end. We accumulate stuff, we accumulate status and we accumulate self-satisfaction. Americans really believe that the one who has the most toys when he dies wins. We equate wealth with what we have accumulated, and so we've received our reward in full.

God calls the church to be different, to find wealth in what we give instead of what we have. I am always amazed at the seemingly effortless knack the early church had for giving to one another as anyone had need. I suppose that part of my amazement has to do with how far away from this ideal we are in the church in America today. Is it possible for the church to live with this kind of generosity again? Our churches need to revive a spirit of generosity. If our churches don't change, how can we expect the world to change? The revival of the church will start with revival in the heart of each follower of Jesus. Will we step out and become an exile in a land of plenty? Will we seek to measure our wealth by what we give rather than by what we have? It has to start somewhere. Why not with you? Why not with me? Why not now?

Discussion Questions

1. Read the following Scriptures: Matthew 5:13-16, I Peter 2:9-10, Luke 15, Matthew 20:1-16. What do these passages tell us about how followers of Jesus are to conduct themselves in such a way that they stand out in contrast to the world?

2. What do you believe was true about the early church that enabled them

---

[1]Mark Buchanan, *Spiritual Rhythm* (Grand Rapids: Zondervan), pp. 132-33.

to give so generously to one another? Read Acts 2:47. What does this verse tell us about the early church and how it was perceived by the world?

3. What are some practical steps today's church can take to become known for its generosity?

4. The idea that "if I give what I have away, I will have less" is pervasive in American culture. Is this idea true? What would God say about this? How does this thinking keep us from being generous with our time, talents and treasures?

5. What are some personal obstacles that hinder us from being demonstrably more generous with our time, talents and treasures?

What's next?

As you close in prayer as a group, ask God to reveal where he wants you to grow in the giving of your time, talent and treasure.

Why not host a potlatch? Invite friends over—make it a small group thing—with the sole purpose of giving things away to one another: treasured things, beautiful things, useful things, rare things.

WEEK 2—GIVING CHEERFULLY

2 Corinthians 8:1-5: *Now I want you to know, dear brothers and sisters, what God in his kindness has done through the churches in Macedonia. They are being tested by many troubles, and they are very poor. But they are also filled with abundant joy, which has overflowed in rich generosity. For I can testify that they gave not only what they could afford, but far more. And they did it of their own free will. They begged us again and again for the privilege of sharing in the gift for the believers in Jerusalem. They even did more than we had hoped, for their first action was to give themselves to the Lord and to us, just as God wanted them to do.* (New Living Translation)

Three armed officers stormed into Amir and Anari's home and proceeded to beat and interrogate them about their faith and church activities in the local village. They demanded at gunpoint that they stop all house church meetings and renounce their faith in Jesus. Amir and Anari remained silent, which infuriated their attackers all the more. After what seemed like hours of abuse, they were murdered in cold blood for not renouncing their faith in Christ.

Over the past two years, Amir and Anari had witnessed many residents come to faith in the Lord, and they were regularly training and encouraging eight house church leaders from the surrounding villages. As the number of converts grew, the local militia felt increasingly threatened and determined to eliminate the threat.

Amir and Anari had willingly left their home country to serve as missionaries in central Africa, both well aware of the dangers they would face. At their commissioning ceremony, they expressed the joy that filled their lives as they reflected on God's love for them and the privilege they had to help others learn of that same hope.

In 2 Corinthians 8, we read of the Macedonians and their "abundant joy" to participate in Paul and Titus' ministry through giving. In fact, it states that "entirely on their own, they urgently pleaded" (2 Corinthians 8:3-4, New International Version) for Paul to accept the gift that was over and above expectation. Now that's cheerful giving!

What caused such a cheerful response? Surely it wasn't because of their circumstances. In fact, this joy came while facing severe trials and the possibility of death. In 2 Corinthians 7:5 we see a glimpse of those trials when Paul shares about his time in Macedonia. He states that their bodies had no rest; they were harassed at every turn and faced outside conflicts and internal fears. Yet, in a way similar to Amir and Anari, they were overflowing with joy and eagerness to share in Paul and Titus' ministry.

What would cause responses like those of Amir, Anari and the Macedonians? The answer can be found in 2 Corinthians 8:5 where it states that the Macedonians "gave themselves first to the Lord" (English Standard Version) and as a result gave themselves fully to the will of God for their lives. When God and his will is our first priority, we can give of our time, talent and treasures and experience the joy only he can provide.

Start today by dedicating your life fully to the Lord and trusting him to transform you into a cheerful giver.

Discussion Questions

1. Have volunteers read out loud the following Scriptures that regard cheerful giving: Exodus 25:2, Deuteronomy 15:10, 1 Chronicles 29:9, 2 Corinthians 9:7, Philemon 1:14. What is God seeking to communicate about our giving?

2. What does it mean to give oneself "first to the Lord"? Invite volunteers to share where they stand in regard to the giving of their time, talent and treasure.

3. Share a circumstance that has prevented you from giving cheerfully. Share what progress has been made (if any), what has helped you grow and what obstacles still exist.

4. Think of someone who models cheerful giving. Briefly share about that person and what draws you to this conclusion about them.

5. How does the gospel demonstrate that God is a cheerful giver? Share evidence from Scripture or personal testimonies. Conclude this discussion by sharing how we are to respond to this wonderful truth.

What's next?

Have each person in the group write down where they have been giving begrudgingly of their time, talent or treasure.

As you close in prayer as a group, confess your heart to God and ask him to help you grow in cheerful generosity, to change your heart and to reveal how to give yourself first to the Lord.

WEEK 3—GIVING SACRIFICIALLY

Mark 10:45: *For even the Son of Man came not to be served but to serve others and to give his life as a ransom for many. (New Living Translation)*

Mark 12:44: *For they gave a tiny part of their surplus, but she, poor as she is, has given everything she had to live on. (New Living Translation)*

In the mid 1950s, Stanley Tam gave control of his business to God by placing fifty-one percent of its stock in a private foundation. If God chose to prosper the business, Stanley would use the profits to spread the gospel around the world. At the time Stanley did this, he was making only fourteen dollars per week! Slowly the business began to grow, and over the years, Stanley realized that perhaps fifty-one percent wasn't enough; perhaps God wanted it all. So eventually he and his wife Juanita made the decision to put one hundred percent of the stock in the foundation. They chose to draw a relatively moderate salary from the business and give all of the profits away.

What was the result of their decision? Over the past half-century, the company has generated over $115 million in profits that have been given away to kingdom work! If you have the pleasure of meeting Stanley Tam today (who is in his 90s), you will find a contented man who has lived a life of purpose—to be used as a tool in God's hand to make money for kingdom work. Surely Stanley has been made rich in every way and lived a life of real prosperity! *(Listen to Stanley's testimony at generousgiving.org/stories)*

The key to giving sacrificially is remembering who we are. We often forget. God saved us from the need to make life work by our own efforts. He saved us from having to fend for ourselves. He saved us from the need to think of ourselves first before we think of others. He saved us from all of this, but we often forget. It's easy to think that we are on our own and that we had better hold on to everything we have. We hold on to our stuff, our time and our resources. We're entitled to it all, right? We have forgotten who we are.

The widow in Mark 12 didn't forget. She knew who she was. When the widow put her two tiny coins in the temple treasury, she was commended by Jesus, and not because her contribution would allow the church to grow exponentially. They wouldn't be able to begin that new outreach program to the orphans with her two tiny coins, or build that new wing for the youth group, and yet, she is the one out of all the rest that Jesus commended that day for her gift. You see, it wasn't about the size of the gift—with Jesus it never is—it was about the size of the giver's heart. With Jesus it's always about the heart.

It's amazing that Stanley Tam turned over his entire business to God, but again, it wasn't about the size of his gift. Stanley Tam could have given the same gift with a wrong heart. The key to the blessings he received was the size of his heart, not the size of his checkbook. Stanley Tam had the kind of heart Jesus could commend, just like the widow. One person's gift was great by worldly standards, the other's not at all, and yet, they were both blessed by Jesus. Both the widow and Stanley Tam knew that true life and blessings come solely from Jesus and by trusting him with everything. They hadn't forgotten who they were at all.

Discussion Questions

1. How does forgetting who we are in Christ cause us to try to make life work on our own power?

2. Describe the line between giving comfortably and giving sacrificially.

3. Why do you suppose God wants us to be sacrificial givers rather than those who give only from our leftovers?

4. How can giving sacrificially become a pathway to greater intimacy with Jesus?

What's next?

Pray together and ask God to guide your group in how he wants you to be more sacrificial.

Email your leader about what God reveals to you throughout the week.

WEEK 4—GIVING REGULARLY

1 Corinthians 9:14: *In the same way, the Lord ordered that those who preach the Good News should be supported by those who benefit from it. (New Living Translation)*

There are only a handful of people you connect with in life who have such a profound impact on your family that it's hard to express. I was reflecting on this as I rode home from church one day with my parents and grandparents in the car. It hit me that there were three generations represented that had been touched by Pastor Hank.

It started over fifty years ago when Pastor Hank led my grandfather to Jesus Christ. My grandfather was a first generation Christian. Pastor Hank took him under his wing and helped him to mature in his faith in the Lord. Pastor Hank helped my grandpa through hard times, including the death of his mom. There were many difficulties during that period and Pastor Hank was always there. Later on, Pastor Hank married my grandma and grandpa and baptized each one of their kids. Over many years, Pastor Hank's teaching and encouragement helped my grandparents to raise a godly family. When my dad was younger, he was also influenced by Pastor Hank. My dad often shares how Pastor Hank would show up at his baseball games just to say hello. He remembers being encouraged in his walk with God and being challenged to take a strong stand for his faith as a teenager when many kids his age were heading in the wrong direction. Pastor Hank was gentle, yet strong, and he truly lived out his faith. He provided counseling for mom and dad before they got married, and I still hear them reflecting on his words of wisdom now and then.

I was born prematurely and spent eight weeks in the hospital. Mom and dad have said that Pastor Hank stopped by several times a week to pray, check up on me and encourage the family. I don't remember this, of course, but it still means a lot to me. Pastor Hank was there when mom and dad dedicated me to the Lord. As I grew older, though his health began to fail and I began to see a little less of him, he still found time to encourage and challenge me in my walk with the Lord.

After church one day I wanted to take the time to thank Pastor Hank for all that he had done over the years for me and my family. When I thought about his fifty years of ministry, I just had to ask him how he could do that for so long. He said, "God has allowed me to minister here for fifty years because of faithful people like your grandparents, parents and many others in this church." I didn't understand what he meant, so I asked for clarification. He said, "Without the faithful ongoing prayer and generosity of the members of this church, I could have never been here this long." I was taken aback by his answer. I thought he would share some leadership tips he had learned over the years that I could apply to my own life. Instead, I found myself leaving that conversation challenged. I was struggling to make it. I had a car payment and insurance and other expenses, so the last thing on my mind was giving to the church. I felt like once again God was speaking directly through Pastor Hank into my life. It was at that point I realized that it was the support of my grandparents and parents that allowed Pastor Hank to make a difference in my life and in the lives of many others. It was shortly after this conversation that I made the decision to start praying for and giving to the church as well, so that the work of Pastor Hank and the other pastors could continue for years to come.

1 Timothy 5:18 says, "For the Scripture says, 'You must not muzzle an ox to keep it from eating as it treads out the grain.' And in another place, 'Those who work deserve their pay!'" (New Living Translation). Are you faithfully supporting your local church and those that minister to you? This is the starting point when it comes to giving.

Discussion Questions

1. Have volunteers read aloud the following Scriptures that regard regular giving: Matthew 10:10, Luke 10:7, 1 Corinthians 9:11-12, Galatians 6:6. What is God seeking to communicate about our giving?

2. Have a volunteer read Luke 8:1-3. How were Jesus and his disciples being provided for? Since Jesus is Lord and owns everything, why do you think he was willing to accept this kind of financial support?

3. Read Romans 12:1-8. What does it mean to be a living sacrifice? How does this relate to the regular giving of our time, talents and treasure within the local church?

4. What obstacles prevent us from giving regularly? Have volunteers share how they have overcome previous obstacles.

5. As a group, share about the individuals who help you grow spiritually. Ask each person to answer this question: "Do you provide material blessings so they can continue to minister in this way?"

What's next?

Ask God throughout the week to reveal the areas where your giving has been sporadic, and how he wants you to become a regular giver.

During the week, share those thoughts with your group leader.

If you are interested in buying 1,000 or more copies of
Ignite Your Generosity in bulk, we can offer a special edition
of the book with your church or organization name
added on the front page of the book.

Bulk discounts are available at
quantities starting at 100 copies.

Please contact our customer contact center at
1-800-843-4587 or at order@ivpress.com
for more information.